THE NEW FOOD GUIDE PYRAMID

Meat and Beans

by Emily K. Green

BELLWETHER MEDIA • MINNEAPOLIS, MN

Note to Librarians, Teachers, and Parents:

Blastoff! Readers are carefully developed by literacy experts and combine standards-based content with developmentally appropriate text.

Level 1 provides the most support through repetition of high-frequency words, light text, predictable sentence patterns, and strong visual support.

Level 2 offers early readers a bit more challenge through varied simple sentences, increased text load, and less repetition of high-frequency words.

Level 3 advances early-fluent readers toward fluency through increased text and concept load, less reliance on visuals, longer sentences, and more literary language.

Level 4 builds reading stamina by providing more text per page, increased use of punctuation, greater variation in sentence patterns, and increasingly challenging vocabulary.

Level 5 encourages children to move from "learning to read" to "reading to learn" by providing even more text, varied writing styles, and less familiar topics.

Whichever book is right for your reader, Blastoff! Readers are the perfect books to build confidence and encourage a love of reading that will last a lifetime!

This edition first published in 2011 by Bellwether Media, Inc.

No part of this publication may be reproduced in whole or in part without written permission of the publisher. For information regarding permission, write to Bellwether Media, Inc., Attention: Permissions Department, 5357 Penn Avenue South, Minneapolis, MN 55419.

Library of Congress Cataloging-in-Publication Data
Green, Emily K., 1966–
  Meat and beans / by Emily K. Green.
    p. cm. – (Blastoff! readers) (New food guide pyramid)
  Incudes bibliographical references and index.
Summary: "A basic introduction to the health benefits of meat and beans. Intended for kindergarten through third grade students."
  Includes bibliographical references and index.
  ISBN 978-0-531-25854-5 (paperback : alk. paper)
  1. Meat—Health aspects—Juvenile literature. 2. Beans—Health aspects—Juvenile literature. 3. Nutrition—Juvenile literature. I. Title. II. Series.
QP144.M43G74 2007
  613.2–dc22   2006000408

Printed in the United States of America.   010111   1185

Table of Contents

Food is **fuel** for your body. Your body needs a mix of healthy foods every day.

You can use the **food guide pyramid** to help you choose which healthy foods to eat.

The Food Guide Pyramid

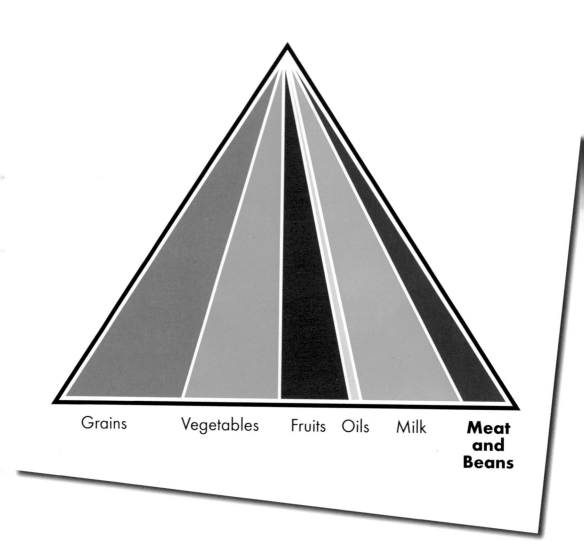

Grains Vegetables Fruits Oils Milk **Meat and Beans**

Each color stripe stands for a food group.

The purple stripe stands for the meat and beans group.

Fish is in the meat and
beans group.

Almonds are in the meat and beans group.

Foods in the meat and beans group have **protein**.

Protein builds strong muscles and bones.

Meat and beans have **iron**.

Iron gives you **energy**.

It is best to eat **lean** meat.

Lean meat is the meat that
is low in **fat**.

Meat **fried** in oil has a lot of fat. Too much fat is not good for you.

16

Beans have very little fat.

1

or

2

Kids should eat one or two **servings** from the meat and beans group each day.

One serving is about the size of your hand. Eat a healthy mix of foods every day.

How Much Should a Kid Eat Each Day?

Vegetables
2½ cups

Meat and Beans
1-2 servings

Grains
6 servings

Oils
5 teaspoons

**Milk, Yogurt,
and Cheese**
3 cups

Fruits
1 ½ cups

Glossary

energy—the power to move

fat—a part of some foods that gives you energy and helps your body use vitamins

food guide pyramid—a chart showing the kinds and amounts of foods you should eat each day

fried—cooked in hot oil

fuel—food that provides energy

iron—a part of some foods that helps your blood to move through your body

lean—the kinds of meat that are lowest in fat

protein—the building blocks in food for your bones, muscles, skin and blood

serving—the amount of a food group that you eat at one time

To Learn More

AT THE LIBRARY

Frost, Helen. *The Meat and Protein Group.*
Mankato, Minn.: Capstone Press, 2000.

Leedy, Loreen. *The Edible Pyramid: Good Eating
Every Day.* New York: Holiday House, 1994.

Rabe, Tish. *Oh the Things You Can Do That Are
Good for You: All About Staying Healthy.* New York:
Random House, 2001.

Rockwell, Lizzy. *Good Enough to Eat: A Kid's Guide
to Food and Nutrition.* New York: HarperCollins,
1999.

ON THE WEB

Learning more about healthy
eating is as easy as 1, 2, 3.

1. Go to www.factsurfer.com

2. Enter "healthy eating" in search box.

3. Click the "Surf" button and you will see a list of
   related web sites.

With factsurfer.com, finding more information is iust a
click away.

Index

The photographs in this book are reproduced through the courtesy of: Phillip Salaverry/Food Pix, front cover; John Giustina/Getty Images, pp. 4-5; Kevin Summers/Getty Images, p. 6; Kelly Cline, p. 7; Stock Food/Getty Images, p. 8; Quayside, p. 9; Sarah Cates, p. 10; Christina Kennedy/Getty Images, p. 11; Rita Maas/Getty Images, p. 12; Alistair Berg/Getty Images, p. 13; Slobodan Ljubisic, pp. 14-15; Andrly Dorly, p. 16; Alex Balako, p. 17; WizData, Inc, p. 18(top); Natalia Clarke, p. 18(bottom); Stuart O'Sullivan/Getty Images, p. 19; Juan Martinez, p. 20(top); Tim McClellan, p.20(middle, bottom), p. 21(bottom); Michael Rosenfeld/Getty Images, p. 21(top); Olga Lyubkina, p. 21(middle).

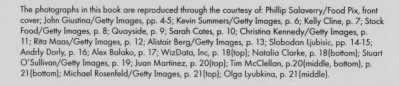